DISPLACED

poems by

Selina Li Bi

Finishing Line Press
Georgetown, Kentucky

DISPLACED

Copyright © 2022 by Selina Li Bi
ISBN 978-1-64662-784-4 First Edition
All rights reserved under International and Pan-American Copyright Conventions. No part of this book may be reproduced in any manner whatsoever without written permission from the publisher, except in the case of brief quotations embodied in critical articles and reviews.

ACKNOWLEDGMENTS

Many thanks to the editors and staff of the following literary journals in which some of the poems in this collection originally appeared:

"Displaced," Cha: An Asian Literary Journal and Red Weather Literary Magazine
"Origin," riksha: Asian American Creative Arts in Action
"Tattooed Girl," riksha: Asian American Creative Arts in Action
"Persimmons," riksha: Asian American Creative Arts in Action

Publisher: Leah Huete de Maines
Editor: Christen Kincaid
Cover Art: Lin Lin, www.visualinlin.com
Author Photo: Tanner Bjorlie
Cover Design: Tanner Bjorlie

Order online: www.finishinglinepress.com
also available on amazon.com

Author inquiries and mail orders:
Finishing Line Press
PO Box 1626
Georgetown, Kentucky 40324
USA

Table of Contents

Displaced 1
Origin 3
Tattooed Girl 4
I'm too busy 5
lies 6
Chrysanthemum Tea 7
Mahjong 8
Amah 9
Persimmons 10
Dutiful Daughter 11
Moon Goddess 12
Kitchen God 13
Old Lady Meng 14
Auntie Po Po 15
Lament 16
My Father Says 17
Snapshots of Manila 18
Hunger 19
I once had an Asian doll 20
The peonies 21
Tai Chi Morning 22
Meditation 23
Compassion 24
Joy 25
Water Dance 26

For my family~
with love and deep gratitude

Displaced

I.
Tonight I burn joss sticks,
sandalwood and lavender
to a porcelain Buddha,
eat sticky rice wrapped in tea leaves,
squid, a fish with jellied eyes.

I suck on dried plums
till the tip of my tongue
bleeds red
like the color on birthdays.
Wear it for good luck, Mother says.

She's a doctor but when I have a headache
she rubs tiger balm on my temples,
says it reminds her of home—
coconut palms, seaweed, and ocean.
It just smells like Vicks VapoRub to me.

II.
Before school, Mother combs my hair
taut into pigtails,
stretching my face like the freckle-faced boys
on the back of the bus,
Chinese, Japanese, dirty knees—
their taunts like a fist in my throat.

Mother says to shut my ears,
not listen to what they say.
She doesn't know how much
my pigtails hurt.

III.
One evening a sparrow
smacked against my window.
I ran outside, found it standing still,
eyes black like shiny marbles.

I clutched the sparrow in my palms,
heart fluttering beneath
its white breast,
wings smooth as the inside
of an oyster shell.

Mother wouldn't let me
bring the bird in the house.
Does not belong here, she said.
Let it go.

I set the sparrow in the grass,
watched it hobble,
wings spread like a paper fan.
I cried as it soared
higher than the trees,
circling beneath the clouds,

where the moon is a pearl
and the sky a silver blue ocean.

Origin

I thought I contracted amnesia
from the Siamese cat next door.

She and I were drunk on sake
when she licked my wound

clean with her rice paper tongue.
I told her it didn't matter—

that I was still trying to forget you.

The way the monsoon rains flood
the streets of Makati in Manila;

barefoot children dance
ankle deep in a sea of brown.

The way a woman tries to forget
the scent of her lover as she returns

home to a bed of plucked orchids,
dried tea leaves steeped

in a cracked porcelain pot, unrecognizable
in the palm of her hand.

The way I forget to look in the mirror
and blush, half-naked,

the smell of burning incense
rising from my navel.

Tattooed Girl

Nothing left but the girl
with persimmon eyes.

A blind immigrant
her fingers trace
the familiar places

on painted flesh
tattooed tongue
bruised black as ink

she shovels words
in her mouth

hands lose touch
over time.

Her face crumples
like rice paper parasols

that stir in the wind
looking for rain.

Absence is color, deep
indelible like her painted scars
unspeakable

like dried plums

like the tiny flame burning
on the tip of her tongue.

I'm too busy

being you

too busy
draped in red silk,
sucking on dried mangoes

too busy
tapping chopsticks
on the drum of my lap

too busy
puckering
like a goldfish
like Mick Jagger

strutting in red stilettos
my hair dyed red

too busy
getting kimchi high.

Better than coleslaw?

The rice porridge simmers.
I add ginger root and scallions
to add flavor, to add fragrance,
to add color.

Tomorrow I'll eat a burger
with my hands,
gulp laughter,

too busy
being you
too busy
being me.

lies

a young girl
clutches her
black umbrella
   waits and waits
for the sea
to eat the sky

clouds
cripple the sun
as she watches
  and waits,
      watches
          and waits.

the sleeves
of her kimono
hide a thousand scars,
deep veins pulse
beneath her skin

and then the lies
and then the lies
she whispers to herself
and then the lies
fall like silk ribbons
        fall like acid rain
           fall like daggers
piercing the belly
of her black umbrella.

Chrysanthemum Tea

Mother takes a pinch
of dried chrysanthemum
steeps it in boiling water,
in a chipped porcelain cup.

Petals unfurl,
faint yellow, soft
like her hands
that cradle the cup
to my lips

edges of petals brown,
like the spots on her cheeks

mine feel a feverish red.

I beg Mother to sing to me
of Yellow River and golden mountains,
plum blossoms,
cherry blossoms,
orchids
their faces to the moon,
but she looks at me
as though she's never heard
of such a song, the melody
too painful, a song best forgotten.

She touches my forehead,
tells me to drink.

I sip
try not to swallow
the flower
as it floats towards the rim.

Mahjong

My aunties sit around the table
playing a round of mahjong.
Tiles click like ivory chopsticks.
Pong, three identical tiles in a row.

They drink jasmine tea,
eat rice cake.
I point to the squares
with Chinese characters.
East, South, West, North.
I only know this
because my mother tells me.

Come join us.
Here, this game
is like rummy.

I feel my face flush
as I shake my head

No.

For I don't know how
to play either game.

Amah

your lips speak
>a language
my tongue
>>longs to know.

As a child
>I buried my face
in the folds
>of your silk dress
tasted ocean
>on your skin
>>in your hair
tangled, salty
>like seaweed
your fingers
>move like waves
>>pulling me further
>>>and further from shore
still searching
>for the oyster shell
still searching
>for the one shiny pearl.

Persimmons

Mother says
the persimmons
are ready to eat.
They have rested—
soft and freckled,
they have rested
no longer tart and crisp.

She cuts one into quarters
like an apple,
her fingers knowing
what they know.
She peels the layer of skin
like a sculptor
not to waste the meat.

Outside the rain
taps a frenetic dance
sideways against the window.
Mother swallows
shadows of the past,
leaving her
stomach empty,
a void I can
not fill.

Lai tsjat,
Mother calls.
Come eat.

I take a slice
of persimmon.

The taste is
not bitter,
but ripe and sweet.

Dutiful Daughter

Spends her life barefoot,
carrying wooden buckets of tofu
on sidewalks littered with cigarette butts
and grease-stained wrappers.
She passes a woman selling duck eggs
dark as ink, nestled in a rusted kettle.

Old men wearing olive green Mao caps
play a game of cards.
Market vendors sell mangoes,
papaya, their seeds
hiding beneath yellow-green skin.

At home, she peels taro,
strips away the hide
to reveal purple flesh,
the knife's blade
dull, a mirror reflecting
a face not her own.

She sees Father's eyes,
Mother's curve of the lip,
their voices
like wings beating
beneath her own breath.

Tonight, she kneels down
in the gaze of the moon,
drinks from the Yellow River,
follows ripples
stretching
longing
to see her own face.

Moon Goddess

A hundred days I mourn for you.
Incense curls to the ceiling
while I burn joss paper and prayer money.
Children fold paper palaces, paper carriages
as if for your afterlife.

I imagine your face
white as talcum powder
smooth as chrysanthemum.

The Emperor's ten sons
blazed the earth,
scorching jade grass to brown—
wilted plum blossoms scatter,
falling in tiny flames
through the chasms of the cracked earth.

From darting arrows, nine sons
plummet to their deaths
and the dismayed Emperor
banished you and your husband
to live as a mortals

but you swallow the pill
of immortality,
your body floats toward evening sky

and on a full moon night
your body shines like a pearl,
melting in the mosaic map of the moon.

Kitchen God
To Zao Jun

I place oranges and pomelos at your altar.
Once you were on your knees, a mortal married to virtue
begging for alms. Love, not only your eyes betrayed.
Blind, you crawl on your belly like a pitiful snake,
hide your face from the moon, a mirror, its edges
cleaver sharp. I should let your insides
bleed a slow death, but you have already
died, your body burned to ash.

I touch your picture,
smear honey on your lips,
but you no longer recognize me.

Ice melts to spring—
a woman washes her hands and feet
in the cold, cold river.

Old Lady Meng
    —Lady of Forgetfulness

gathers herbs
from lakes and streams
to protect the souls of the dead.
Her legs bend like bamboo,
fingers gnarled as she scoops
bittersweet broth.

One sip of her five flavored tea
and all memory will fade,
all past lives lost
of who you once were.

Auntie Po Po

Sweet and salty aromas fill the room,
which means she's cooking.
Cleaver in one hand,
fingers of the other ready to hold down
   strips of raw beef
        green scallions, garlic.

Her eyes are slits in steam,
strands of black hair fall, shiny
like a crow's wing,
a splintered fan
before her eyes.

Blinded with the smoke
   of sizzling scallions,
        browning bits of garlic
she hollers, **Open windows, quickly!**

I watch as plumes of smoke escape,
faces of ancestral ghosts.

We eat in silence,
except for the smack of our tongues
swallowing memories of back home.

Lament

Mother braids my long, black hair.
In the mirror, I watch her fingers
twist and untwist,
tucking in
every loose strand.

She holds a rubber band
between her teeth
and tells me
how she once had hair
like mine,
how she wished
she'd saved the ivory clip,
the one that held
the dark cocoon
on the back of her head.

I close my eyes
and in my dreams
she pulls the ivory claw,
hair unfurling
like a silk curtain
down her back.

Tears like rain
fall on my pillow
as she sways to the music—
her fingers strumming air
her fingers strumming air.

My Father Says
       Cebu, Philippines 1942

He was not afraid
when the Japanese soldiers
knocked on their door
and ransacked
their nipa hut
by the sea.

He was not afraid
of the incessant sound
of guns firing.
He ran to the highest hill,
watched the planes
fly overhead.

Engines roared
angry like fire
across the sky.

He was not afraid
when evening arrived
and only the moonlight
guided their way
as they left their home,
heading toward the mountains,
walking barefoot along
the seashore
footprints
sinking in the sand.

I was not afraid,
my father says.
I was just a child.

Snapshots of Manila

I remember the brown-skinned girl,
long black hair flowing down her back.
She places a lei of sampaguita flowers around my neck.
Its sweet fragrance, like perfume, rises up my nostrils.

Mabuhay, she says in Tagalog. Welcome.

Kalesa rides down broken streets,
the clip-clop of a weary horse,
its tail swinging side to side
brushing off flies
sticky as honey.

A bright orange and silver jeepney
swerves past, honking its horn.

Street vendors sell mangoes, papayas, and bananas.
A barefoot boy wanders between cars,
tapping at windows,
waving Marlboro and Winston cigarettes for sale.

I remember the monsoon rains
flooding the streets.
Cars float like boats on a river.

I splash in puddles knee deep,
my sandals drifting away without oars.

Hunger

I saw it this morning
in the eyes of a beggar—
the one sitting akimbo,
the one catching flies
with his tongue
flicking out like a frog,
waiting for pesos
to drop from the sky.

I once had an Asian doll

I pressed her tummy
and she coughed up
red beans, sweet mooncake.

I tore off her arms, her legs,
watched her spin a cocoon
like a silkworm,
fine threads she pulled
from the sky.

One night she grew wings—
her eyes fluttered
as I pried open her mouth.

I wanted to see if I could taste
the sliver of moon,
razor sharp
on the partial eclipse
of her tongue.

The peonies

      hide their faces
in young jade bulbs
      swollen, waiting for the sun
to touch their aching bodies
      satin lips unfurl
a fan of white and pink flesh
      blush like rice paper lanterns
a fury of hungry ants
      drowning in sweet nectar.

Tai Chi Morning

A blue heron lifts its leg—
white crane spreads its wings
as sunlight breaks
through morning clouds.

A sparrow sweeps
along a stony path
by a lake
where a man
moves slowly

hips turning to the left
turning to the right
with the wind
with the air

breathing in breathing out

arms circle
high and low
forward and backward,

palms open and close
smooth as ink strokes
amidst gray sky,
capturing shadows.

Blood flows—
moving chi
yin and yang,

where nothing else matters,
just movement and light
movement and light.

Meditation

My mind is a forest
of persimmon rain
as I hang from the branch
of a Bodhi tree
and watch the Buddhist monk
as he sits akimbo
wrapped tight in a saffron robe.

He is not waiting or wanting,
only listening to the birds
flapping their wings,
breaking through
the silence
like the sun
as it slices
through the forest
like the thick foliage
like the damp canopy
like the air
like the jungle
awakening.

Compassion

It seems so simple—
my hand to my heart
but here I feel the pulse
of the little bird,
wings beating
ready to take flight
as I breathe in for me
and out for you,
in for me
and out for you.

Joy

I long to gallop
like the wild blue horses
as they chase the moon on open prairie.
Hooves touch the dry earth,
leaving clouds of dust in their midst.

See how they pause and listen
as they reach the forest—
where the air smells sweet
of Moonflowers
and the trees speak
their wisdom through the wind.

Don't be afraid, they whisper,
to allow your broken heart to open.

Don't be afraid
to allow your broken heart to flutter.

For the stars above
shimmer and wait for you
to drink the painted sky.

Water Dance

All I need
is a drop of rain
to forget you.

The orchids
hide their damp faces
from the blue moon
that awakens
the wind
the blue moon
that awakens the lake
of your knowing.

A hungry trout
rises to the surface
fireflies tap dance
above ripples
of water
and the blue moon
awakens
untouched
and lonely
no more.

With Thanks

I'm deeply indebted to Alan Davis, Kevin Carollo, Lin Enger and my other writing instructors and mentors at Minnesota State University Moorhead MFA Program: Mark Vinz, Liz Severn, Shari Scapple, Thom Tammaro. You guided, inspired, and gave me a safe place to explore my voice. I'm forever thankful for your support.

Sincere thanks and gratitude to my dear writing friend, Sarah Beck, for your keen eye and insight, artist Lin Lin for your beautiful work, my agent, Linda Camacho at Gallt & Zacker Literary Agency, Denise Lajimodiere, and everyone at Finishing Line Press.

My deepest gratitude to my family: Kevin, Kayla, Mason, Shakes & Mandi, and especially Tanner, for your creative expertise and endless help and support on this project. I'm extremely thankful and appreciative to my mom and dad and my sisters for their love and support.

Selina Li Bi was born in Philadelphia, Pennsylvania, to immigrant parents from the Philippines and was raised in North Dakota. Growing up, she and her sisters gathered at the dinner table, listening in awe as their father and mother told stories about their homeland, sharing a trove of memories, treasures from the past.

She later studied biology and earned a Doctor of Optometry degree from Pacific University in Forest Grove, Oregon. After practicing as an optometrist for many years, she earned an MFA in Creative Writing from Minnesota State University Moorhead. It was during this time that she began to explore her identity and Asian roots. Writing became a journey of self-discovery, an exploration of the dichotomy of cultures in which she was raised.

Selina currently lives in North Dakota. She is a daughter, a sister, a wife, and mother of three emerging adults. Two loyal pups are her writing companions while running and yoga keep her grounded. She believes art has the power to connect, inspire, and awaken one's sense of belonging in this world.

Website: www.selinalibi.com

www.ingramcontent.com/pod-product-compliance
Lightning Source LLC
LaVergne TN
LVHW041511070426
835507LV00012B/1489